Learning About Your Health

Fever

By

Kenneth T. Burles

ROURKE PRESS, INC.
VERO BEACH, FLORIDA 32964

Printed in the United States of America.

Library of Congress Cataloging-in-Publication Data

Burles, Kenneth T., 1946-
    Fever / Kenneth T. Burles.
        p.   cm. — (Learning about your health)
Summary: Discusses the nature, causes, and treatment of fever and explains that it is the body's way of fighting infection.
    ISBN 1-57103-256-8
    1. Fever—Juvenile literature. [1. Fever]   I. Title.
II. Series: Burles, Kenneth T., 1946-   Learning about your health.
RB129.B872   1998
616'.047—dc21

                                                                                        98-7654
                                                                                        CIP
                                                                                        AC

Photographs: Cover, pp. 5, 9, 14, 15, 19, 22, © PhotoDisc; pp. 10, 11, 17, © Adobe Systems Incorporated; pg. 21, © Digital Stock; pg. 25, ©RubberBall Productions.

Contents

How Do You Feel?

You wake up and feel hot. You throw off the blanket. You feel cold and have chills. You are thirsty and want a drink of water. You do not feel well. You have a **fever** (**fee**-ver).

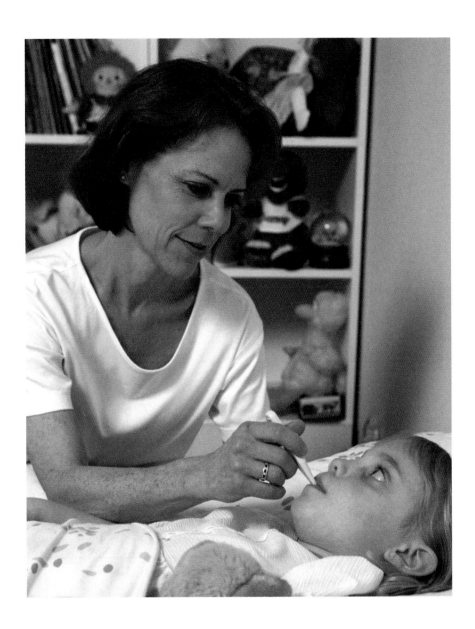

What Is Fever?

Hippocrates (Hi-**paw**-krat-ease) lived in ancient Greece. He is called the father of modern medicine. He once said "Give me a fever and I will cure all disease." Most doctors today agree with him. A fever can signal nature's healing process.

The word "fever" comes from the Latin word "favere." It means "to warm." Fever is when your body temperature (**tem**-per-ah-chur) rises. It lets you know something is wrong with your body. You may have a cold. You may have the flu. You may have a virus (**vy**-russ).

What Is Temperature?

Temperature is how we measure hot and cold. You can measure the temperature of the air outside or inside your house. You can also measure the temperature of your body.

How Do You Know Your Body Temperature?

Your body temperature should be 98.6 degrees Fahrenheit (**fair**-en-heit) or 37 degrees Celsius (**sell**-c-us). You measure your temperature with a thermometer (ther-**mom**-me-tur).

You must not drink a hot or cold drink 15 minutes before taking your temperature. You put the thermometer under your

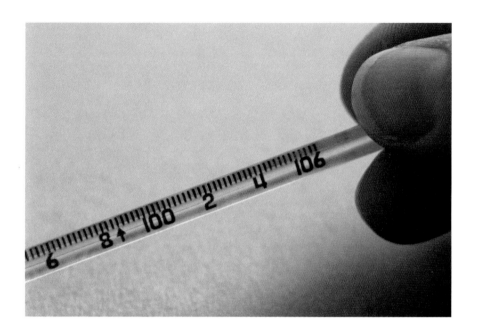

tongue. You keep your mouth closed and remain still. You should not bite the thermometer. You remove the thermometer from your mouth about three minutes later. You read the numbers on the thermometer.

The numbers tell you how high your temperature is. Temperature can be a little higher or lower than 98.6.

What is a Thermometer?

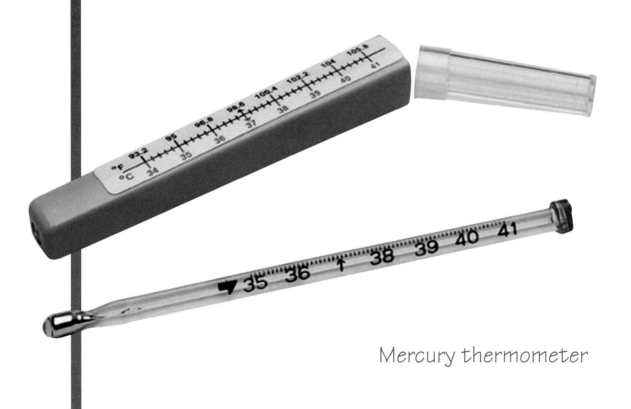

Mercury thermometer

A thermometer measures temperature. You can hang a thermometer on the wall of your house to see how warm or cold it is outside. You can put an oral (**or**-all) thermometer under your tongue to measure your body temperature.

There are glass mercury (**mur**-cure-e) thermometers and digital (**digh**-it-all) thermometers to measure your body temperature. A digital thermometer is easy to read. It shows only the numbers of your temperature.

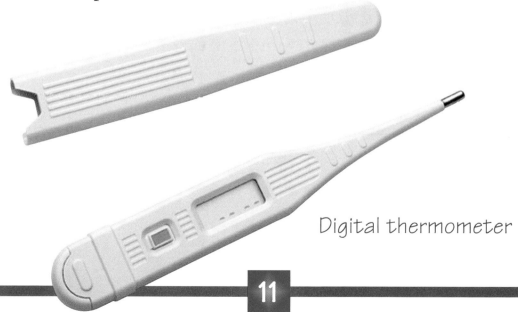

Digital thermometer

Fahrenheit or Celsius?

There are two scales, or series of numbers, that tell us how hot or cold something is. On the Celsius scale, water freezes at 0 degrees and boils at 100 degrees. A single number in the scale is a degree. It is often shown with the symbol °. On the Fahrenheit scale water freezes at 32° and boils at 212°.

CELSIUS   **FAHRENHEIT**

water boils **100** ——— **212**

water freezes **0** ——— **32**

What is Normal Temperature?

There are cold-blooded animals and warm-blooded animals. Snakes are cold-blooded animals. They use the outside temperature to change their body temperature. A snake lays in the warm sun to raise its body temperature.

Humans are warm-blooded. We use energy released when we digest food to keep our body temperature normal. Doctors often call normal body temperature the body's "set point."

You can set your heater at home with a thermostat (**ther**-moe-staht). You choose a temperature. The heater stops when the room reaches that temperature. It begins to heat the room when the temperature falls below that temperature.

Like snakes, lizards use the warm sun to raise their body temperature.

Setting Your Thermostat

Like your heater at home, the body has a thermostat. It is in your brain. It controls your body's set point. When the weather is hot, it sends more blood to the skin and you perspire (purr-**spire**). When the perspiration dries you feel cooler.

When it is cold, it sends less blood to the skin and makes the muscles contract (kon-**trakt**) to increase heat. When you have an infection (in-**feck**-shun), the

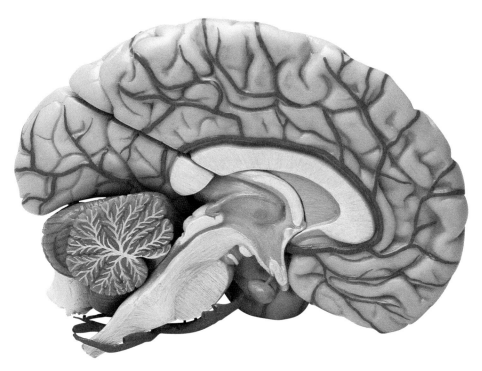

Your body's thermostat
is located in the brain.

autonomic nervous system (auto-**nahm**-ick **ner**-fuss **sis**-tem) gets a signal and increases your body's set point. Your brain makes a fever to fight the infection.

Fever
Good or Bad?

Fever is usually good. It is how the body fights infection. Viruses or bacteria (back-**tear**-e-uh) cannot live when your body turns up the heat. When the infection is gone, your body's thermostat will make you sweat. This cools your skin and lowers your temperature.

When you have a high fever, you should visit the doctor. The doctor does not worry about the fever. He wants to find out what causes the fever.

Children should not take aspirin when they have a fever.

You can have a high fever with flu or other viruses. Viruses cause colds, chickenpox (**chik**-en-pocks), and other illnesses. Medicine cannot help some illnesses. You must wait until the illness runs its course.

What Do I Do When I Have a Fever?

You might not eat much when you have a fever. You must drink a lot of water or juice. You should dress in light clothes or pajamas. If you get chills, you can wrap in a blanket. Another way to cool the skin is to soak in a bathtub of water at room temperature. The water draws heat from the body. These are not cures. They are only ways to feel better until the illness is over.

It is important to drink a lot of fluids like juice and water when you have a fever.

What To Do
If You Have
a Fever

- **Take your temperature.**

- **Drink plenty of liquids.**

- **Rest.**

- **Dress lightly.**

- **Take a pain relief medicine.**

- **If your temperature is above 103° or lasts more than 3 days see a doctor.**

The Fever Pattern

Think back on the last time you had a cold or the flu. You begin to feel bad. Then you become warm. You have a fever. You want to be warm and quiet. You don't eat much. You drink water often. Next you begin to sweat. That signals that the fever is "breaking." When your fever "breaks," or returns to normal, the illness is gone. You begin to feel better. You will want to rest to become strong again.

When fever begins
stay warm and
quiet.

What Do Doctors Think?

Most doctors think that temperature is good. It is a natural way to fight illness. You only need to visit the doctor if your temperature is very high, if you have other symptoms, or if your fever lasts more than three days.

C.A.L.M.

Parents often worry when a child has a fever. C.A.L.M. is a guide for parents from the Association for the Care of Children's Health.

✓ **C**heck your child's temperature.

✓ **A**ssess other signs and symptoms your child may have.

✓ **L**ower the room temperature to make your child more comfortable.

✓ **M**onitor you child's behavior and temperature.

Glossary

bacteria (back-**tear**-e-uh) - germs that cause infections in your body.

Celsius (**sell**-c-us) - the scale used to measure temperature in the metric system. Water freezes at 0° and boils at 100°.

chickenpox (**chik**-en-pocks) - an illness caused by a virus

contract (kon-**trakt**) - when muscles contract they become shorter and tighter.

degree - one number in a scale to measure temperature is a degree.

digital (**digh**-it-all) - showing a read-out in numbers. A digital clock shows only the number for the time at the moment.

Fahrenheit (**fair**-en-heit) - the scale often used to measure temperature in the United States.

fever (**fee**-ver) - the body temperature rises because of an infection.

mercury (**mur**-cure-e) - a silver colored liquid used to measure temperature in a thermometer.

oral (**or**-all) - having to do with the mouth.

perspire (purr-**spire**) - you perspire or sweat when you are warm to cool your body. The moisture on your skin dries and your body feels cool.

temperature (**tem**-per-ah-chur) - how hot or cold your body or the air is.

thermostat (**ther**-moe-stat) - the control that keeps a heater at a set temperature.

virus (**vy**-russ) - a germ that causes an infection in your body.

For More Information

Children's Healthwatch from Mayo Clinic. http://healthfront.com

Grolier Encyclopedia of Science and Technology. Danbury, CT: Grolier Educational Corporation, 1994.

Health Infopark. http://www.merck.com

Kingfisher Children's Encyclopedia. New York: Kingfisher Books, 1992.

Raintree Steck-Vaughn Illustrated Science Encyclopedia. Austin, TX: Steck-Vaughn, 1997.

Rourke's World of Science Encyclopedia. Vero Beach, FL: Rourke Corporation, Inc., 1998.

The World Book Encyclopedia. Chicago: World Book, Inc., 1998.

Index